with jesus

31 DAYS OF GROWING IN RELATIONSHIP

Tyler Sollie

WITH JESUS
31 Days of Growing in Relationship

ISBN: 9798843186791

DEDICATION

This book is dedicated to everyone who has been a voice in my life to take a step forward in following Jesus.

It is also dedicated to those who are ready to take that step for themselves.

My hope and prayer is that in the following pages, you would see Jesus a little more clearly, and that through those moments, your life will experience transformation that would move you to share that same hope with someone else.

THANKS

I want to thank the Life Center Board for allowing me space to write and create resources that will help people take steps forward in their journey with Jesus. I am thankful for your commitment and passion to *bring life in Jesus to every life in our communities.*

Thank you to my Executive Leadership Team, Pastors, and Staff of Life Center Church for your prayer, encouragement, and support.

Thank you to the people of Life Center. Thank you for being the church that you are, committed to Jesus and seeing the impact and transformation we can make as we partner with Him on His mission.

Thank you JB, Sarah, Tasha, Brooke and others who helped in the reviewing and editing of this book.

Finally, thank you to my family. You truly are my first and most important ministry. Amber, Judah, Justus, and Faith – you make life rich. I hope that you will find joy and encouragement in these words. I am thankful that our family is in this together.

My life passion is to KNOW JESUS & MAKE HIM KNOWN. I hope and pray that this book is a helpful tool in that direction for every individual who picks it up and works through the pages.

INTRODUCTION

Thank you for taking time to lean in to a 31-day journey that has the ability to transform your life. I know that those words sound like a big claim…and they are. But as you will soon discover, the words that we are going to look at over the next 31 days are anything but common or ordinary. I believe they have the power *to change everything*. And I'm not alone in this. There are millions of people throughout the centuries that have had the trajectory of their lives altered because of the significance of the words that we will be spending time with. The most important element: the source of where these Words came from.

There have been many important people who have walked the face of the earth throughout history. People have left their impact on fans, foes, and followers. There have been powerful people who left their mark on the pages of history. Others are remembered because of heroic sacrifice or incredible works of compassion and care. But of all the important and even famous people that have lived, none seem to stack up against a carpenter turned teacher from a small town called Nazareth. His name: Jesus.

What was it about Jesus?
How was it that He could take a group of twelve students and literally shift the trajectory of mankind?

How could this man gather thousands of people to listen to His words, and over 2,000 years later, those words are still impacting lives?
Why were his followers so committed to keeping and documenting His words…

I believe it is because Jesus is so much more than a historical teacher. He is far more than someone who started a movement, did some good deeds, or healed people and performed miracles. Jesus is more than an example that we look to so that we can add inspiration to our lives to "become better people". Jesus came for a cause and a purpose much more than these things.

Years ago I heard a statement about Jesus that had a deep impact on my understanding of who He is and why He came.

> ***Jesus did not come to make bad people good. He came to make dead people live.***

This is why I am so excited for these next 31 days together. We get to listen to the Words of Jesus – the One who came to bring LIFE. Our greatest need isn't just to get a little better or do more good. Our greatest need is to receive the Life that He alone provides. We have the opportunity to experience life *With* Jesus.

As we will discover over the next 31 days, His words will encourage us, challenge us, confront us, comfort us, convict us, inspire us, and amaze us. But my prayer for you is that it will do more than that. My prayer as I write this, is that you will come to encounter *LIFE* through His Words. That His Life will transform *your life*.

Before we begin, I want to ask you to commit to spending time each day over the next 31 days to show up ready to meet with Jesus. Set aside the distractions for a few minutes. Set your phone to "Do Not Disturb". Grab a cup of coffee. And put yourself in a space where you are not just reading the Words of Jesus, but you are positioning your heart to *encounter* the One who spoke these Words.

Again, thank you for taking time to engage in this journey. I am confident that as you lean in, you will discover that Jesus has already been moving toward you in preparation for this moment.

Tyler Sollie

Senior Pastor
Life Center Church
Tacoma, WA

A PRAYER

Before we begin this 31-day journey, I want to invite you to pray the following prayer out loud with me. For those who have never prayed or feel like you're "*not good at that prayer thing*", I want to remind you that it is simply a conversation with God. Talk to Him and with Him like you would with a friend.

Jesus,

I am taking these next 31 days to listen to and learn from Your Words. Help me throughout the days ahead to not simply read, but also to listen and consider how you are speaking to me today. I want to create space to encounter You as I hear and process Your Words. Give me ears that would hear. Give me eyes that would see. Give me a heart that would understand. I give you permission to speak to me, Jesus. Comfort me where I need comfort. Challenge me where I need to be challenged. Convict and correct me where I need it. Encourage and inspire me where I need it. I want to hear Your words and discover Your heart.

Thank you that You are with me.
Thank you that You are for me.
Thank you, Jesus, that You love me.

Amen

THE DAILY PROCESS

This book is designed to be used daily over the course of 31 days, to create a rhythm of hearing Jesus' words, reflecting on His truth, discovering His heart, and engaging in a few practices so that we can live the transformed lives that He makes available through His grace.

This book is designed for those who are new to faith in Jesus, as well as for those who have been following Jesus for a while and want to take some intentional time to reflect on His words.

Each of the days will follow a similar rhythm to help you listen to the words of Jesus, apply its truth, put His words in context of what is taking place in scripture as He is saying them, and have the opportunity to engage in some practices to help drive truth deeper into our hearts and minds.

Each day will include:

> **WORDS OF JESUS**
> **A SHORT DEVOTIONAL THOUGHT**
> **THE DAILY PRINCIPLE**
> **THE DAILY PRACTICE**

My hope and prayer as you engage in this journey is that Jesus would become more beautiful to you, and that you would be amazed that His word is alive and is for you *today*.

If this journey is helpful to you, share this book with someone else. Maybe take a friend through it with you who isn't yet a follower of Jesus. Maybe you want to use this as a family resource, to create conversation with your kids about Jesus and how He wants to work in and through our lives.

I have been praying for you, that this time would have an incredible impact and that together our faith will be strengthened as we spend 31 days together, hearing Jesus' words and discovering His heart.

With Jesus

DAY
ONE

"THE" IS GREATER THAN "A"

"I am the way, the truth, and the life. No one comes to the Father except through me."

(Jesus speaking to his disciples in **John 14:6**)

Here's the deal – there are a lot of opinions out there about Jesus.

> *Good teacher on wisdom and a non-violent ethic*
> *Exemplary moral example*
> *Miracle worker*
> *Noble humanitarian*
> *An ancient teacher turned martyr at the hands of Rome*

History proves that there is an actual man who lived in ancient Israel named Jesus. People don't tend to argue about that. Most people will affirm and agree that He was a *good* historical figure who did *good* things.

But the tension shows up in what Jesus actually claimed about Himself, and what His followers believed and taught about Him. And as we start this 31-day journey together, hearing and reflecting on the actual words of Jesus and as we move to experience His heart, there is an important truth that serves as our starting block:

WHAT YOU BELIEVE ABOUT JESUS IS AND WILL BE THE MOST IMPORTANT THING ABOUT YOU.

What Jesus claims about Himself in John 14:6 has massive implications *if* we take Him seriously. Notice His Words – He makes a claim. A statement that gives us the option to either embrace or reject what He is saying. If I'm honest with myself as I consider these words, He doesn't leave me a third option or a middle ground.

Jesus says, "*I am the way, the truth, and the life. No one comes to the Father except through me.*"

Jesus doesn't say that He is *a way* among many ways.

Jesus doesn't say that He is *a truth* or has *some truth*.

Jesus doesn't offer an *addition to your life*.

He simply, yet profoundly, states that He is it. He's THE WAY, THE TRUTH, THE LIFE.

You might say, "well that is His opinion". But you can't disconnect what He said about being the way, the truth, and the life from what He says next.

In these eighteen words, Jesus makes an exclusive claim. Here is the problem with exclusivity – it feels offensive, especially to those who don't want to embrace it. Jesus takes His claim to another level when He says we actually can't get to the Father except *through Him*.

Here, Jesus is actually addressing mankind's greatest need going back to when things went horribly wrong in Genesis 3. Scripture's starting point is the truth that there is a good God, who set into motion a good creation and a good plan. But something went horribly wrong.

Humanity rebelled against God (which is what the bible calls sin), and it fractured their ability to walk with God. From that point, God set into motion His new plan that would *undo* what sin had done to His good creation.

What was that plan?
Jesus.

He accomplished for us what we could never accomplish for ourselves. I can't work, earn, or deserve my way into relationship with God. So God clothed Himself in humanity (what we call the *incarnation*). He lived, died, and rose from the dead for us.

So don't miss the significance of what Jesus is speaking to you today.

He is THE WAY, not just a way.

He is THE TRUTH, not just a truth among many truths.

He is THE LIFE, not just a hopeful or helpful improvement to the life you have.

Receive that.

Rest in that.

DAILY PRINCIPLE:
WHAT YOU BELIEVE ABOUT JESUS
IS THE MOST IMPORTANT THING
ABOUT YOU.

DAILY PRACTICE:
CONTEXT: *Put Jesus' Words in context
by reading* **John 14:1-11**

REFLECT:
*What things stuck out to you from
today?
What do you sense Jesus speaking to
you about right now?*

PRAY

With Jesus

DAY
TWO

FOLLOW ME.

"Follow me."

(Jesus speaking to Matthew when he was at his tax
booth in **Matthew 9:9**)

Have you ever felt overlooked?

Elementary school can be a challenging time,
especially at recess. One memory still sticks
with me from a kickball game. Two captains
had all of the kids line up on the fence. This is
a test of resolve for kids. There is one thing
you definitely do not want to be: picked last. I
remember that moment all too well, hearing
names called and starting to get nervous. I was
hoping that I wouldn't be overlooked. I was
hoping that someone would not only see me,
but choose me. What a relief when my name
was finally called.

Maybe you have had a moment where you
thought you were forgotten about, overlooked,
or not valued. Most of us have had some kind
of experience where we felt like we were on
the outside, looking in.

I think there are many people who feel that way
about God.

Some may think, "I know there is a God…but I
don't think I'm His type of person." "What would

He want with someone like *me*?" You may have even been told by others that God would never accept or love someone like you. Maybe you have been told that He loves some people, but not people like *you*.

There is something so striking about Jesus' interaction with Matthew. Because of his occupation, Matthew should have been off limits. He was a tax collector for Rome, the foreign empire that was oppressing the people of Israel. And Matthew was working for them! He should have been a cast aside or a cast out.

But not to Jesus. Two words were spoken that day to Matthew that completely changed the trajectory of his life and His destiny:
Follow Me.

I want you to think about those two words.

Follow Me.

Here are a few things to consider. First, all of us are following *something*. This word follow means to come behind, keep in step with, or pattern your life after. All of us are following something. But there is a better way. Not *something* new to follow, but rather *Someone* to follow. Second, I want you to consider the second word: "**Me**". This was Jesus' invitation. Notice that he didn't call Matthew to follow an ideal or an ideology. He didn't invite Matthew to follow a new trend or a cultural value system. He called Matthew to follow *Him*. What does it mean to actually *follow Jesus*?

Some of us are simply moving too fast to follow. Our pace is not in alignment or conducive to allow Him to lead us, so we settle for adding a little of Jesus to our lives, instead of laying down our life to follow Him. Others maybe like the usefulness of Jesus, but don't want to deal with the pressure or cost of actually *following*. Some might joyfully follow, but feel like they are not in a good enough condition yet to be welcomed into that space. Your story might look a little different, but the reality for each of us is the same: He invites us to *follow Him.*

But a word of caution. Don't think for a moment that your following Him is on *your terms* or *your agenda*. He loves you – no doubt about it! But part of following is the decision to lay aside the ability to call the shots.

Here is what I mean: some of us like "Savior Jesus" and "Grace Jesus" – but we can't forget that He is also and always "Lord Jesus". He calls the shots.
The invitation is available.

Those two words, *follow me*, still have the power to change everything.

How will you respond?

DAILY PRINCIPLE:
AM I FOLLOWING JESUS ON HIS
TERMS OR MY OWN?

DAILY PRACTICE:
CONTEXT: *Put Jesus' Words in context
by reading* **Matthew 9:9-13**

REFLECT:
*What things stuck out to you from
today?
What do you sense Jesus speaking to
you about right now?*

PRAY

With Jesus

DAY
THREE

HE IS GOOD AT IT.

"I am the good shepherd. The good shepherd lays down his life for the sheep."

(Jesus, speaking to a crowd in **John 10:11**)

What are you *good* at?

Seriously. Take a moment and answer that question.

Often, it is easier for us to focus on what we are *not* good at. But all of us are good at something. Some of us are strong with people and relationships. Others are good in areas of strategy and logistics. The list is nearly limitless when it comes to the variety of strengths that people have in their lives. But when we focus on this level of "good" we almost always focus on a skill, talent, or ability.

Consider Jesus words in John 10:11. He doesn't just say He is *good at shepherding*. He says He is the good shepherd. He isn't drawing attention to a specific skill or ability. He is telling us about His character. He is revealing something important to us.

He is a *good shepherd*.

33

Since most of us live life in the modern west, this example and its significance can be lost on us. When we hear these words, we probably have little more than an image of someone standing in a pasture, watching sheep. This is accurate, and it is also incomplete.

Think for a moment of the implications of Jesus telling us that He is our good shepherd.

A shepherd keeps a focused watch on his flock.

This matters because it means that Jesus, being our good shepherd, *sees you*. He knows you, and is aware of where you are at. Jesus has His eyes on you. I know for some that can sound scary or even threatening – but put that idea in context. Just as a shepherd who is caring for a flock, watching with focus and intentionality, Jesus keeps a focused watch on us.

A shepherd protects the flock from danger and enemies.

This matters because it means that Jesus is committed to our safety and protection. He was and is willing to take on our enemies. He was and is willing to protect us from danger. There are things that the shepherd understands and sees that the sheep can't or won't. Jesus is our protector.

A shepherd makes sure the flock is fed and taken care of.

This matters because it means that Jesus is going to provide for you. A good shepherd doesn't neglect their sheep, they provide for them. Jesus, our good shepherd, will make sure that we are taken care of. He cares about your entire life because you are valuable to Him.

A shepherd makes sure to lead and guide the flock to the best location.

This matters because it means that Jesus is going to lead you to a place that is best for you. A shepherd had a responsibility to make sure they took the sheep to places where they could feed and flourish. Jesus is no different. He wants us to come to the place that He sees as best and that we would follow His lead and His direction there.

Think about Jesus being *your* good shepherd. Listen to these words from a young shepherd in the Old Testament. He understood something about God seeing him, protecting him, providing for him, and leading him.

> "*The* L*ORD* *is my shepherd; I have what I need. He lets me lie down in green pastures; he leads me beside quiet*

35

waters. He renews my life; he leads me along the right paths for his name's sake. Even when I go through the darkest valley, I fear no danger, for you are with me; your rod and your staff— they comfort me. You prepare a table before me in the presence of my enemies; you anoint my head with oil; my cup overflows. Only goodness and faithful love will pursue me all the days of my life, and I will dwell in the house of the LORD as long as I live."
(Psalm 23, CSB)

DAILY PRINCIPLE:
AM I TRUSTING JESUS AS MY GOOD SHEPHERD?

DAILY PRACTICE:
CONTEXT: *Put Jesus' Words in context by reading John 10:1-18*

REFLECT:
What things stuck out to you from today?
What do you sense Jesus speaking to you about right now?

PRAY

,

DAY
FOUR

FAMILY BUSINESS

"Didn't you know that it was necessary for me to be in my Father's house?"

(Jesus speaking to His parents in **Luke 2:49**)

I grew up the son of a small business owner. My dad was the visionary for his company, the finance director for his company, the labor for his company, the marketing as well as customer service director for his company. He did it all. From a young age I started going to work with him, "helping" him where I could. As the years would pass, my awareness of how things worked and of understanding how my dad would want things done became second nature to me.

In Luke chapter two we get our only glimpse into the life of Jesus as an adolescent – He was twelve years old. These are the first "red letters" (words spoken by Jesus), that the Gospel writers give account of.

Picture the moment: Mary and Joseph had traveled to Jerusalem for the festival. They depart with a large group of family members and friends who are traveling back to their home city of Nazareth. They assume that Jesus is with them in the crowd. After a days travel they realize that Jesus isn't with them

41

and they rush back to Jerusalem to find their misplaced Son (imagine being responsible for misplacing God…).

Three days later they find Jesus in the temple in Jerusalem listening and interacting with the religious teachers. When His mother asked why He did this, His response is somewhat striking: *"Why were you looking for me? Didn't you know that it was necessary for me to be in my Father's house?"*

It's almost as if Jesus is reminding both His parents as well as us of something that we shouldn't lose sight of: He is sent from the Father on assignment. Even as a young boy, He had awareness of His purpose and call. Even at age twelve, He understood the necessary dynamic of obedience to what the Father's purpose was for His life, His mission, and His ministry.

What does this mean for us?

First, recognize that Jesus' work for us was intentional. You were not an afterthought or a mistake. In fact, God in the flesh – even at twelve years old – was committed to the purpose of the Father that was revealed all the way back in Genesis when He promised to break the curse that sin had created for mankind. Jesus had an awareness of purpose – and part of that purpose included you.

42

Second, don't miss the importance of the community and unity that is displayed between the Father and the Son. Jesus was so much more than a good teacher, a miracle worker, or the pioneer of a new religion. Jesus is God in the flesh. He is the Son, was committed to the work of the Father, and released the gift of the Spirit into the hearts of His followers. Theologically this idea is called "Trinity" which means "three in one". We believe in One God who has expressed Himself in three persons completely unified: Father, Son, and Spirit.

These first words of Jesus are a reminder to us of the commitment to God's purpose being fulfilled. Jesus' work was intentional, and His commitment for me and you was seen even as a twelve year old who understood the business He was a part of.

That is something that we can take comfort in.

DAILY PRINCIPLE:
JESUS' WORK FOR ME WAS
INTENTIONAL.

DAILY PRACTICE:
CONTEXT: *Put Jesus' Words in context by reading* **Luke 2:41-52**

REFLECT:
What things stuck out to you from today?
What do you sense Jesus speaking to you about right now?

PRAY

DAY
FIVE

HE IS WILLING

"I am willing; be made clean"

(Jesus speaking to a man with leprosy desiring to be
healed in **Luke 5:13**)

In Luke 5 there is a shocking interaction that
takes place between Jesus and someone in
need. To appreciate the dynamics in this story,
it helps to understand the social realities of the
day. There was a number of things in ancient
culture that had the ability to make someone a
social outcast. A lapse in moral uprightness
could land you on the outcast list quickly.

Another issue that had the ability to impact
your social dynamic is a physical condition that
would deem you "unclean". There were certain
and specific religious and ceremonial laws that
would dictate whether or not someone needed
to live separate in order to keep disease from
spreading to others. One such issue is the
catalyst of the interaction with Jesus in Luke 5:
a man who had a skin disease called leprosy.
Now before we go further, let me ask you an
important question:

**If you were to rate God's level of
willingness to help you, how would
you score it?**

Some of us carry an idea or picture of God that is simply not accurate. We assume that God has to tolerate us out of duty. We imagine a subtle eyeroll as we bring our real conditions and challenges to Him as He says under His breath, "All right… let's get this over with." But notice how Jesus *actually* responds to what most looked as an outcast, an untouchable, a problem to be avoided. Jesus says, "I am willing."

Those words spoken to that man were probably more than enough. But what takes place beyond the words is critically important. Scripture says that before Jesus even spoke the words, He reaches out His hand and *touches him*.

Jesus touches the untouchable.

This was problematic because under Old Testament Law, the mans "impurity" should have transferred to whoever touched him, making them unclean as well. But do you see the difference here? Jesus is revealing that something has changed with His arrival and His key message that the Kingdom of God is here.

Don't miss this:

Instead of the uncleanness of the man impacting the cleanness of Jesus, it was actually the holiness of Jesus that transformed the uncleanness of the man with leprosy.

This has massive implications for us.

You may see yourself as unworthy and unclean.

You may believe that you don't deserve God's kindness to deal with whatever has made you "unclean" in life.

You may wrestle with the willingness of God, believing that maybe He tolerates you and has to put up with you because…well, He is God.

Jesus reveals something radically different about God.

Remember He is the visible representation of who God is and how He loves (Colossians 1:15).

Reflect on this:
There is nothing that you can't bring to Jesus that He is unwilling to deal with. There is nothing in your life that His healing power can't redeem and restore. While others may have cast you out or cast you aside, Jesus wants to reveal life to you.

What is it today that needs to encounter His willingness?

DAILY PRINCIPLE:
> THERE IS NOTHING THAT JESUS IS
> UNWILLING TO DEAL WITH THAT I
> BRING TO HIM.

DAILY PRACTICE:
> **CONTEXT**: *Put Jesus' Words in context*
> *by reading* **Luke 5:12-14**
>
> **REFLECT**:
> *What things stuck out to you from*
> *today?*
> *What do you sense Jesus speaking to*
> *you about right now?*
>
> **PRAY**

DAY
SIX

OUR COMMON SICKNESS

"It is not those who are well who need a doctor, but those who are sick. I didn't come to call the righteous, but sinners."

(Jesus speaking to religious leaders who were upset that He was spending time with "sinners" in **Mark 2:17**)

Jesus is full of surprises. This is what kept frustrating and agitating the religious leaders of His day. He kept doing things that appeared to be a radical departure from the status quo. With the words that He spoke and the actions He took, it kept grinding against the long standing perspective of how things were supposed to be.

But Jesus didn't come to maintain the status quo.

He came with a purpose.

In Mark 2 we read about the time that Jesus encounters a man named Levi (whose name will later become Matthew). Here is the problem: Levi is an outcast. This is because Levi has chosen an occupation that makes him an enemy to his fellow people: he is working with the foreign oppressor, Rome and collecting taxes for them.

People in this line of work were cut off. They were traitors. They were no good. Everyone knew that. It seems like everyone understood the social implications…except Jesus.

As Jesus is walking He sees Levi sitting at his tax booth and Jesus does the unthinkable as a rabi (teacher). He invites Levi to "follow" Him. Jesus actually invites *that guy* to become one of His students. To learn His ways. To pattern His life after His way of teaching and living. Clearly this would have cause questions not only for the religious leaders watching all of Jesus actions and interactions, but His disciples would have also had some questions about His decision.

The next glimpse we get is Jesus is at a party at Levi's house. Jesus is there, in the middle of the action with – other tax collectors and "sinners". Those who were cast out by others, Jesus is actually spending time with them. Not to become like them, but to welcome them into the *life* that He is making available. As we reflected on yesterday, Jesus' influence was and is enough to make the unclean *clean*. When the religious leaders saw what was taking place, they questioned Jesus about His actions and methods.

Don't you understand what kind of people you are surrounding yourself with?

If you were truly holy and from God, you wouldn't spend time with people like them.

But Jesus, well aware of His mission, states something so important: He came as a doctor for those who are sick. The religious were certain that *they* didn't have a sickness – it was all "those" people.

But Jesus words cut to the heart: all of humanity shares a common sickness. Rebellion against God. *Sin*. And He came to undo what our sin has done.

Here is what I know – all of us have a level of brokenness in our lives. Some of us are just better at hiding it than others. We all have a common sickness, and there really is only *one* cure: **Jesus**.

And the same Jesus that was willing to touch the man with leprosy, is the same Jesus who is willing to deal with our sickness.

DAILY PRINCIPLE:
> ALL HUMANITY SHARES A COMMON SICKNESS THAT JESUS CAME TO HEAL.

DAILY PRACTICE:
> **CONTEXT**: *Put Jesus' Words in context by reading **Mark 2:13-17***

> **REFLECT**:
> *What things stuck out to you from today?*
> *What do you sense Jesus speaking to you about right now?*

> **PRAY**

DAY
SEVEN

GET TO WORK

"This is the work of God—that you believe in the one he has sent."

(Jesus speaking to a large crowd in **John 6:29**)

Growing up the son of a painting contractor, I had the opportunity to start going to work with my dad at a young age. Most Saturdays and school breaks, I would be heading out to jobs with him, "helping". As I look back now, I realize that especially when I was young, I probably was creating more work than less. Yet over time, I began to understand what the work was and how to engage in it.

Many people, when they think about following Jesus, start with work.

What do I need to *do*?
What do I need to *change*?
How do I live *different* now?

Though these questions may be good, they are both incomplete *and* off target.

Notice that all of the questions center around *them*. They are not God focused, they are self-focused. This matters, because our salvation isn't a reward for our work or our effort (see Ephesians 2:8-9). Following Jesus is not

59

rooted in our effort or work to get ourselves cleaned up or work our way to a good relationship with God. If that were true, it would make us the saviors – and we could take credit for being or becoming "good".

But let's be honest: even on our BEST days, we still need grace. And here is some good news: even on your worst days, you're not outside of the REACH of grace. This is because you have a strong and sufficient Savior named Jesus. He has already done for you what you could never do for yourself. Change isn't rooted in our effort. Change is rooted in what Jesus has done for us. So where does *work* come in?

Jesus made it clear the most important work He has given us: TO BELIEVE. More specifically, to believe in Him. Not just believe that He existed, but to believe that He is our only hope, our only source of life and salvation. He is the only one who can make us clean and new – forgiven and free. And it is from this place of *belief* that we put that *belief to work.*

Remember, Christianity isn't against working – it's against trying to earn salvation. If I truly *believe* in Jesus, it will be seen in how I live my life out (see Ephesians 2:10). I am not working *for salvation*, I am working *from the salvation that I have received in Jesus.*

So where does that bring us today?
It's time to get to work. Not working to get
yourself to God – that will never happen
through your own effort.

It is time to get to work in *believing*.

Believe that Jesus loves you.

Believe that Jesus lived and died and rose
again for you.

Believe that He is the only source of life and
freedom and forgiveness.

Believe that He wants relationship with you and
that He invited you into deeper believing today.

DAILY PRINCIPLE:
THE WORK WE START WITH IS
BELIEVING JESUS.

DAILY PRACTICE:
CONTEXT: *Put Jesus' Words in context
by reading **John 6:22-29***

REFLECT:
*What things stuck out to you from
today?
What do you sense Jesus speaking to
you about right now?*

PRAY

DAY
EIGHT

OPEN IT UP AND MAKE IT YOURS

"Peace I leave with you. My peace I give to you. I do not give to you as the world gives. Don't let your heart be troubled or fearful."

(Jesus speaking to his disciples in **John 14:27**)

I love receiving gifts. I think we all do. I am blessed to have some incredibly thoughtful friends who are kind, thoughtful and generous. They rarely miss giving a gift. I can tell that they actually love *giving* gifts.

Every now and then I think back to some of our kids first Christmas'. I remember the excitement that I had about some of the things we had wrapped up and placed under the tree for them. We were both excited and expectant about the moment they would open the gift and enjoy it!

But something strange happened.
On more than one occasion, I remember giving the gift to my kids, watching them with excitement and anticipation remove the wrapping paper and play with it…*and not even open the box to receive the real gift inside.*
I know that I'm not the only person that has experienced the strange dynamic of this moment: the gift is within their grasp, but they don't even open it up and make it their own.

Consider Jesus' words to His disciples. Jesus is well aware of His approaching death. He knows that in a matter of days, His closest friends – those that He chose to carry the message of His life, death and resurrection were going to be discouraged and disheartened.

To these individuals (as well as to us), Jesus gives them a promise and a gift that brings hope.

Jesus said that He was giving them peace.

Not just any peace.
His peace.

Let that sink in. Jesus didn't say that He was going to provide circumstances where *our* peace would finally show up because we are content. He said that He was going to give His disciples *His peace*. This has the ability to change so much in our lives. Think about all of the moments that you *lack* peace. Think about all the times that you wish you had peace.

Jesus said that He has given us His peace. He reminds those original disciples as well as us today to not allow our hearts to be troubled. How can you face that challenge at work and not lose your hope? **Because you have received Jesus' peace.** How can you journey through a challenge in your physical health and not be overcome by anxiety? **Because you have received Jesus' peace.** How is it that we can remain hopeful in chaotic or stressful circumstances in this world in which we live? **Because you have received Jesus' peace.**

But don't miss this: even though Jesus offers it, we have to receive it and open it up and make it ours. Don't make the mistake that my kids made when they took the wrapping paper off, but didn't open the gift. You heard Jesus' words: "I give you peace."

Now open it up, receive it, and make it yours!

DAILY PRINCIPLE:
> TO EXPERIENCE THE PEACE OF
> JESUS WE HAVE TO RECEIVE IT,
> OPEN IT UP, AND MAKE IT OURS.

DAILY PRACTICE:
> **CONTEXT**: *Put Jesus' Words in context
> by reading **John 14:27-31***
>
> **REFLECT**:
> *What things stuck out to you from
> today?*
> *What do you sense Jesus speaking to
> you about right now?*
>
> **PRAY**

DAY
NINE

ALL THINGS?

"...but with God all things are possible."

(Jesus speaking to his disciples in **Matthew 19:26**)

Are you facing something in your life right now that seems like an *impossibility*?

You have prayed, and nothing has changed. You have hoped, and things are the same. You have tried to believe and have faith that things can be transformed...but the impossibility remains.

Maybe you have been there. Maybe you are there now.

In the conversation that Jesus is having with His disciples, a wealthy man had just walked away from Jesus sad. Jesus tells His students that it is hard for those who are rich to enter the Kingdom. The disciples are shocked by this statement and this line of thinking. In their culture, riches were a sure sign of God's blessing and His approval and favor. They are left to wonder, if the rich are going to have a hard time, then who on earth can possibly experience salvation?

Jesus makes a simple statement that has massive implications.

"With man this is impossible, but with God all things are possible."

That is a big statement.

All things, Jesus? That must be a metaphor or something, right? *ALL things?*

Here is the point: we don't always see things as God sees them. What may appear impossible to you *IS* possible for God.

If we really understood this, and really believed it, think about how that would change your day to day living. Think about how that would change how you approach prayer. Think about how that might adjust the way you sing and worship when you understand you are actually singing to the King of the universe who can do *all things*.

What is hard for us is not hard for God.
What is beyond expectation for us is well within His power and ability.

What seems well beyond reality is in His grasp.
What is impossible for us *is* possible for Him.
Let that sink in as you face your day today.
There is nothing outside of His power, strength, or ability. All things are possible for God.

If you are in relationship with Jesus, you are invited to come boldly to that same God with your needs (see Hebrews 4:14, Ephesians 3:12).

What may be impossible for you, is not an impossibility for God!

DAILY PRINCIPLE:

THERE IS NOTHING OUTSIDE OF
THE STRENGTH, POWER, OR
ABILITY OF JESUS.

DAILY PRACTICE:

CONTEXT: *Put Jesus' Words in context
by reading **Matthew 19:23-30***

REFLECT:

*What things stuck out to you from
today?
What do you sense Jesus speaking to
you about right now?*

PRAY

DAY
TEN

TELL HIM

"What do you want me to do for you?"

(Jesus speaking to two blind men who called out to get
His attention in **Matthew 20:32**)

Have you ever had the experience of trying to
get someone's attention, but no matter how
hard you tried it seemed like their focus would
never come your direction?

*A busy waiter during a lunch rush at a
restaurant.*

*A spouse or child who just won't break
attention with their phone.*

*A customer service representative who
never wants to let you off of hold on that
phone call.*

Moments like that leave you feeling that if you
could simply get their attention, things would
be better. I believe there are many people who
believe they have to work hard to get the
attention of God. They tell themselves things
like, "with so many people in this world, God is
probably too busy to deal with someone like
me." Or, "after what I did last week, I doubt
God would ever want to give me the time of
day again…"

But take a moment to reflect on what Jesus says to two blind men who call out to Him in order to get His attention. At one point the crowd had told these men to be quiet, but the kept on calling out to Jesus. And a crazy thing happens: He not only hears them, He calls them over and asks them this question, "What do you want me to do for you?"

Now there is something important that we cannot forget about Jesus: He is God. And what that means is He already knows what the men *want* and *need*.

So why does Jesus invite them to tell Him? As you read through the scriptures about Jesus, He often asks people what it is that they need.

Maybe you're a little like me. At times, you know that God "knows", so why should I say anything if He is already aware?

Why should I pray or ask God for something if He is all knowing?

Here is a crazy thought for today: Jesus *wants* to hear from you.

Seriously.

The King *wants* to hear from you.

He isn't annoyed by you, sick of you, or rolling His eyes at you.

If He had a phone and you called Him, He wouldn't send you to voice mail.

Yes, He is aware of what you already need, but He invites us into relationship with Him as we follow Him. We are welcomed to communicate, to talk, to share and express what is going on. So, what are you waiting for?

Tell Him. Right now. Right where you are at. With your own words. No fancy language is needed – Jesus invited you today with a similar question and invitation: *What do you want me to do for you?*

DAILY PRINCIPLE:
> JESUS WANTS TO HEAR FROM YOU.

DAILY PRACTICE:
> **CONTEXT**: *Put Jesus' Words in context by reading **Matthew 20:29-34***
>
> **REFLECT**:
> *What things stuck out to you from today?*
> *What do you sense Jesus speaking to you about right now?*

PRAY

DAY
ELEVEN

BE AWARE

"Watch out that no one deceives you."

(Jesus speaking to a small group of His disciples in
Mark 13:5)

Have you ever been tricked?

I'm not talking about getting one of those trick
pieces of gum or candy that taste like some
ridiculous thing. I'm talking about being full on
duped. Years ago, it was time for us to get a
new car. We were so excited to find a great
deal in the newspaper (remember those?) on a
newer model car that was exactly what we
were looking for. We made the call, went and
looked at it, even took it for a test drive. We
couldn't believe the deal that this individual
was making for us to have this car.

Why was the price so good?

We found out that it was a salvaged car that
had been totaled. Here is the problem: we
found out *after* we had made the purchase. If
you have ever heard of the phrase "stupid tax",
this is where it came from.

What made that moment so frustrating was
that we didn't know we were being deceived.
We thought what was being sold to us was
good, authentic, and a great deal.

This is exactly how deception works. If you *knew* that it was deception, you wouldn't take it.

Jesus wanted His disciples to be aware that deception is a possibility…for all of us. Even as disciples. Even as people who know Jesus and engage with scripture. Deception can still happen.

You may say, "not me."

Maybe you are convinced you are too smart, too mature, too discerning, or too spiritual to be deceived. But consider Jesus words for a moment.

He tells them to "watch out".

Be on guard. Be aware. Be vigilant.

Why?

Because all of us are not only *capable*, but we are also *susceptible* to being duped.

We believe that taking the shortcut and sacrificing our integrity won't matter.

We believe that the little things don't add up. We convince ourselves that we are the best sources of truth and avoid any voices that will lovingly confront or correct us in areas that we need it.

We know that others are capable of being deceived, but we have grown past that point. These words from Jesus are a sobering reminder that we are all still dealing with this shared human condition. Deception has been the enemy's tool since the beginning in the book of Genesis.

Here is the point: just because it looks good, doesn't mean it is good.

And because Jesus loves us so much, He gave us a warning to be on guard against it.

DAILY PRINCIPLE:
WE ARE CAPABLE OF BEING
DECEIVED.

DAILY PRACTICE:
CONTEXT: *Put Jesus' Words in context
by reading **Mark 13:1-8***

REFLECT:
*What things stuck out to you from
today?
What do you sense Jesus speaking to
you about right now?*

PRAY

DAY
TWELVE

DEEPER IS DOING

"Why do you call me 'Lord, Lord,' and don't do the things I say?"

(Jesus teaching a large crowd in **Luke 6:46**)

As a pastor, I can't tell you how many times I've heard people say they want to go "deeper". These comments usually center around their desire to explore topics or scriptures that they believe are "deep" and will lead them to a greater place of understanding and knowledge. I get it. I love to learn new things and gain new insights too. I love it when I have one of those lightbulb moments where new insight, truth, or revelation hits my heart and mind.

But here is the subtle danger that we don't often recognize when it comes to this line of thinking: deeper isn't just adding more information to our lives.

In fact, I believe our world would be transformed if followers of Jesus simply lived out and put into practice what they *already know*.

The challenge for many of us isn't that we lack information. In fact, we live in a time in history where we have access to more information than any other generation that has lived. In

89

addition to this, we have access to scripture and biblical resources with a simple swipe on our phone. But with all this information, are we really going *deeper*?

Jesus was teaching a large crowd along with His disciples. He was talking about life in His Kingdom and what it should look like. He wraps His teaching with a picture of what *deeper* actually looks like. He challenged His listeners to not call Him "Lord", and then not implement and do what He has asked them to do. Their issue wasn't in their hearing. They *heard* Jesus' teaching. It seems that the disconnect, according to Jesus, was their willingness and ability to *do* what He said.

Here is the truth: you can access and listen to the greatest teaching. You can podcast, read, audiobook, Google, and social media yourself into non-stop biblical content. And here is the danger: you can *convince yourself* that you are going "deeper".

But if the "deeper" isn't revealed in the *doing*, I would argue that you have added information – but that information hasn't yet led to transformation.

Deeper is *doing*.

It is putting into motion what Jesus has taught us to do.

It is not only believing He is life (John 10:10), but also embracing and living out His way of life.

I am convinced that sometimes the greatest thing that will lead us to experience transformation is simply acting on and putting into motion the things that we have already learned and know.

This doesn't mean we stop learning. I know for myself, I want to be a life-long learner. The key is to avoid the trap of believing we just need to "go deeper", when in reality many of us need to discover that deeper is *doing*.

DAILY PRINCIPLE:
GOING DEEPER IS REVEALED IN
THE DOING.

DAILY PRACTICE:
CONTEXT: *Put Jesus' Words in context
by reading **Luke 6:43-49***

REFLECT:
*What things stuck out to you from
today?*
*What do you sense Jesus speaking to
you about right now?*

PRAY

DAY
THIRTEEN

DON'T STOP READING

"For God did not send his Son into the world to condemn the world, but to save the world through him."

(Jesus in a conversation at night with Nicodemus in
John 3:17)

I'm guessing that at some point you have seen a sign with the following statement on it:

JOHN 3:16

From endzone shots at a football game, to a street corner near you, you have more than likely seen this mixture of letters and numbers that serve to direct people to an important truth: God's Love. From that famous verse in scripture, we grow to understand that God *loves* the world – so much so, that He sent Jesus who is His one and only Son. I love this verse and the truth that it declares to our lives!

I remember being a kid in church and memorizing bible verses. John 3:16 was one of the very first bible verses that I put to memory. I am thankful for people who helped me at a young age learn important truth from scripture.

I also wish I had kept reading after verse 16. In the very next sentence, Jesus tells Nicodemus why He was sent. Nicodemus was a Pharisee – a group of religious leaders among the Jewish people who were known for their legalism and their condemning approach to humans who didn't measure up to their strict moral code.

I wonder how many people view Jesus, not through His words or actions, but through the words and actions of people who claim to follow Him?

Jesus pointed this Pharisee to the truth that God loved the world so much that He wanted to save the world. Jesus was His great rescue plan.

Maybe today, you are feeling condemnation over decisions you have made or mistakes that are piled up in the rearview mirror of your life. Today, you might be convinced that you are the exception to what Jesus said.

Pause for a moment, right where you are at, and read the following out loud a few times. In the blank put your first name:

> *"For God loved _____ in this way: He gave his one and only Son, so that everyone (including _____) who believes in him will not perish but have eternal life. For God did not send his Son into the world to condemn*

_____, *but to save*
_____ *through him."*

God loves you.

Jesus came so that you didn't have to be
condemned. We have all fallen short and
messed up, but because of Jesus and through
Jesus – new life is available (Romans 3:23,
Romans 6:23). Freedom, forgiveness, a new
start – all because God loves you and Jesus
came so that you wouldn't be condemned, but
so that you would be saved.

DAILY PRINCIPLE:
> JESUS CAME SO THAT I WOULDN'T
> BE CONDEMNED.

DAILY PRACTICE:
> **CONTEXT**: *Put Jesus' Words in context by reading* ***John 3:1-21***
>
> **REFLECT**:
> *What things stuck out to you from today?*
> *What do you sense Jesus speaking to you about right now?*

PRAY

DAY
FOURTEEN

NO EXPIRATION DATE

"Heaven and earth will pass away, but my words will never pass away."

(Jesus speaking to a small group of His disciples in
Mark 13:31)

I know that we are all wired a little different. Some of us are natural risk takers, while others of us are wired to play it safe at all costs. Some reading this are willing to push things right up to the limit, while others of us like a little more margin and safety.

There are many activities that I love to do that some would consider risky.

> Rock climbing
> Backcountry skiing
> Surfing
> Jumping off of elevated objects into the water

There are a few things, however, where I don't like to push the limits. One thing in particular that I become a little obsessive about: expiration dates on food. I think it all goes back to a bad experience I had when I was a kid, and for those who have weak stomachs, I will spare you the details. Because of that experience, if something is even close to being expired, I tend to not want anything to do with it.

Here is some good news for people like me: Jesus' words do not have an expiration date. So many people believe that because something is *old* it might not be relevant any longer. But today, I want you to consider the truth that Jesus is speaking: this world and everything you know will pass away, and His words will still remain.

They are eternal.

They are lasting.

That means that the same hope that the crowds experienced as He spoke can be your hope today. His words still remain. They will last the test of time. The truth of His words that He loves you, cares about you, has a purpose and plan for you, are as real today as they were when He walked the face of the earth with His disciples.

Here is what this provides in our lives today: confidence.

We can be confident as we grow to know Jesus and know His words that they will come to pass. They are truth that we can count on and build our lives upon. There are many things in our world that will come and go.

Styles come and go.

Trends come and go.

Influencers come and go.

Pop culture comes and goes.

But the words of Jesus will remain forever. Let that build your confidence today. In a fresh way, set your hope, joy, and peace in what Jesus has declared about you and for you!

DAILY PRINCIPLE:
JESUS' WORDS HAVE NO
EXPIRATION DATE.

DAILY PRACTICE:
CONTEXT: *Put Jesus' Words in context by reading* **Mark 13:28-31**

REFLECT:
What things stuck out to you from today?
What do you sense Jesus speaking to you about right now?

PRAY

DAY
FIFTEEN

SIX WORDS THAT CHANGE EVERYTHING

"It is I. Don't be afraid."

(Jesus speaking to His disciples in **John 6:20**)

Fear is a powerful motivator.

In recent years, we have seen the impact that fear and concern can have on people and society. I remember being at a conference a number of years ago and the question was asked, "What would you do if you had no fear of things not working?" It's a powerful question. Many of us have had moments of opportunity, only to be held back by fear of the unknown or all of the "what-ifs" about outcomes that we can't really control.

One thing we all must be aware of: fear has the ability to form our lives.

If left unchecked, fear becomes the motivation under our decisions and our direction in life. Here is the good news: Jesus doesn't want you to live motivated by fear. Fear no longer has to be the master of your decisions, direction, or motivation in life.

> *Will I have enough?*
> *Am I enough?*
> *Am I truly loved by God?*

Am I secure?

I want you to take a moment and reflect on the six words that Jesus spoke to His disciples who were in a boat on a lake during a storm. Maybe that is a good description of where life has been, or even is right now for you. The wind and waves of strife, anxiety, uncertainty, or frustration are stirring around you.

Take a moment to hear and consider six words of Jesus:

"It is I. Don't be afraid."

Jesus doesn't tell them that they don't need to be afraid because *their* wisdom is going to pull them through. He doesn't imply that the antidote to their fear is the fact that they are in a boat that is seaworthy. Jesus doesn't point them to hope in their efforts or hard work to transform the situation that they currently find themselves in.

Instead, Jesus reassures and reminds them He is there. At first, they are concerned about the wind and the waves. After rowing a few miles in these conditions, there is a second thing that unnerves them: someone or something is walking toward them...*on the water*. The opportunity to panic, to freakout, to be greatly concerned is theirs. Yet to their fear, Jesus redirects their attention and their focus with six words.

It is I.
Don't be afraid.

Where do you need to be reminded today that Jesus is not only aware of what you are walking through, but He is actually there with you? What is the circumstance that you need to be reminded of His presence by receiving those same six words?

Today, reflect on those six words. Think about how the fact that Jesus is here, right now – it actually changes *everything*.

DAILY PRINCIPLE:
JESUS ISN'T JUST AWARE OF WHAT YOU ARE FACING, HE IS WITH YOU IN IT.

DAILY PRACTICE:
CONTEXT: *Put Jesus' Words in context by reading **John 6:16-20***

REFLECT:
What things stuck out to you from today?
What do you sense Jesus speaking to you about right now?

PRAY

DAY
SIXTEEN

HOW TO LOSE AT WINNING

"For what does it benefit someone if he gains the whole world, and yet loses or forfeits himself?"

(Jesus speaking to His disciples in **Luke 9:25**)

I enjoy winning. I am guessing you do as well. In fact, I'm not sure that I have ever met someone who actually *enjoys* losing. There are some who are addicted to winning, and there are others who can lose and hold their composure. But deep down, each of us in our humanity want to know that we have come out on the winning side.

We do this even in the little things, don't we?

Which line will be the fastest at the grocery store?

Which lane should I get in at the stop light so I can pass that individual?

How soon can I get the new device when it is released?

How can I prepare my response in this argument (even though I have to neglect to listen to the other person) just so I can win?

We all like to win.

It's not wrong to win. And I don't think it is even wrong to *want* to win.

The problem is when we begin to "win" in the wrong things, or in the things that actually don't matter.

Jesus gave His disciples an important warning. He let them know that it was possible to win, and in winning they would actually lose. He warned them about the temptation to "gain the whole world". Most of us wouldn't describe what we are setting out to do as *gaining the whole world*, but pause for a moment and ask yourself an honest question: **what is the bullseye for your life?**

If you received everything that your time, effort, money, and desire are aiming at, *would it actually be success?* And if it is a success, it's a success according to *whom*?

Today is an opportunity to reflect and consider what you are actually aiming your life at. You can gain many things – but if you lose your soul in the process, you have lost at winning. No matter what culture or society tells you, winning is not:

More possessions

More followers on social media
More money in the account
More power or position or popularity
More accolades

None of these things are wrong or bad in and of themselves. But how many people do you know, or how much time have you spent in your life trying to amass these things? Jesus gives us a warning because He loves us.

You could win at all of the things that this world says is valuable and important…and still lose. Today, consider what the actual bullseye is that your life is aimed at. If it is anything other than Jesus and His purpose and plan for you, allow Him to adjust your direction.

DAILY PRINCIPLE:

IT IS POSSIBLE TO WIN AT WHAT
THE WORLD SAYS IS IMPORTANT,
AND STILL LOSE.

DAILY PRACTICE:

CONTEXT: *Put Jesus' Words in context
by reading **Luke 9:23-27***

REFLECT:
*What things stuck out to you from
today?*
*What do you sense Jesus speaking to
you about right now?*

PRAY

DAY
SEVENTEEN

KEEP IT REAL

*"Whenever you pray, you must not be like the
hypocrites, because they love to pray standing
in the synagogues and on the street corners to
be seen by people. Truly I tell you, they have
their reward."*

(Jesus speaking to a crowd of people in His "Sermon on
the Mount" in **Matthew 6:5**)

I tend to like things that are authentic. What
about you?

Nothing really compares to the real thing. No
doubt you have experienced substitutes and
fakes in your lifetime. From breakfast cereal to
cookies and beyond, many of us remember a
time where someone gave us something – and
even though it *looked* like the real thing, it
wasn't the *real thing*.

One of the things that often brings me hope
and joy is the fact that God welcomes us to
bring our authentic self to Him. He isn't looking
for the highly filtered or airbrushed version of
us. He wants us to bring the real thing. This
includes how we approach relationship and
conversation with Him.

Conversation with God – what we often call
prayer – tends to be intimidating to people. I
can't tell you how many times I have had

people tell me that they "are not good at prayer". This often shows up whenever I am at a dinner party or lunch with people and they will look at me and say (because I am a pastor), "Will you pray over our meal?"

I'm thankful for the opportunity to pray, but I also wish that more followers of Jesus understood that it isn't about having fancy words or even well-constructed sentences. God simply desires authenticity.

He wants you to keep your conversations with Him real.

Take a moment and reflect on Jesus' teaching on prayer from Matthew 6.

Notice a few things:
1. **Jesus expects us to pray.**
   Notice that He says, "When you pray…"

2. **Jesus expects us to be real.**
   He specifically says don't be like the hypocrites.

3. **Jesus expects us to check our motives.**
   He is calling out people who were praying in public to be seen by people. They are putting on a show. They have the look, the sound, maybe even some

fancy words…but the problem is it lacks authenticity.

Prayer is such an amazing privilege. We *get* to spend time in relationship talking with the King of Kings. We get to share our needs, worries, doubts, fears, failures – we also get to share our worship, our thanks, our awe, and our praise to the only One who is truly worthy.

Today, practice bringing your authentic self into conversation with Jesus. It's not about the amount of words, or even all of the "right" words, just be you.

For those that are new to following Jesus, and the thought of talking to someone you can't see, give this a try:

It is a simple prayer model – and to help you remember it, just think **T.A.C.O.S.**

Start by **THANKING** Jesus for what He has done for you.

Then move to **ADORATION**, expressing why you love Jesus.

Then **CONFESS** anything you need to be forgiven of.

Then pray for **OTHERS** and the needs that they have.

Finally pray for your **SELF** and the needs that you have.

Take a few minutes today, bringing your authentic self to Jesus and have a conversation with Him. And no matter what you say, just keep it real.

DAILY PRINCIPLE:
> BRING YOUR AUTHENTIC SELF TO
> JESUS AND HAVE A
> CONVERSATION.

DAILY PRACTICE:
> **CONTEXT**: *Put Jesus' Words in context
> by reading* **Matthew 6:5-15**

> **REFLECT**:
> *What things stuck out to you from
> today?*
> *What do you sense Jesus speaking to
> you about right now?*

PRAY

With Jesus

With Jesus

DAY
EIGHTEEN

REAL REST

"Come to me, all of you who are weary and burdened, and I will give you rest."

(Jesus speaking to crowds of people in **Matthew 11:28**)

One idea that we have pointed to a number of times in the journey of this book is the idea of "resting" in a truth about Jesus.

Today is going to be a simple reflection and exercise.

Look at Jesus' words. Consider their significance.

Come to me

There are many places we go to find relief and rest. Maybe your favorite thing to retreat to is your bed, a good meal, a vacation spot, or one of your favorite activities that recharges you. Maybe the place you go to find relief is less ideal: an escape through distraction, numbing yourself through over eating or drinking too much, a return to an addiction that seems to comfort for a moment but then leaves you empty.

When Jesus calls us to come to Him, it's not some form of escape – it's actually a return to real life since He is the source of life. Jesus doesn't start with a list of things for those who are weary and burdened. Instead, He offers Himself.

Let that sink in. He starts with an invitation to come to Him.

Who does He target this invite to?

All those who are weary and burdened

No matter who you are, where you are from, or your specific occupation, it is safe to say that you feel the ache and the burden and the weariness of living in a culture that goes 24/7. If you have been weary, you are weary, or you sense weariness is in your future, this invitation is for you.

Here is the promise that Jesus offers:

I will give you rest

Jesus doesn't offer you a cheap substitute. Jesus doesn't give you a distraction. Jesus offers us something that each one of our souls desperately needs: real rest.

I love Eugene Peterson's paraphrase of Jesus words from The Message Bible:

"Are you tired? Worn out? Burned out on religion? Come to me. Get away with me and you'll recover your life. I'll show you how to take a real rest." (Matthew 11:28, The Message)

So here is the exercise:

Go to Jesus. Right now. If it is 90 seconds you have, give Him the next 90 seconds. If you have 10 minutes, give Him the next 10 minutes.

Don't go a step further in your day today without first answering the invitation that Jesus has extended to you and for you.

Real Rest.

DAILY PRINCIPLE:
>JESUS DOESN'T OFFER YOU A CHEAP SUBSTITUTE; HE OFFERS REAL REST.

DAILY PRACTICE:
>**CONTEXT**: *Put Jesus' Words in context by reading **Matthew 11:25-28***
>
>**REFLECT**:
>*What things stuck out to you from today?*
>*What do you sense Jesus speaking to you about right now?*

PRAY

DAY
NINETEEN

HOW TO MEASURE LIFE

"Watch out and be on guard against all greed, because one's life is not in the abundance of his possessions."

(Jesus speaking to a crowd in **Luke 12:15**)

One of the things that I haven't been able to outgrow is the joy I get in sneaking up on people and startling them. There is something about my stealth approach and their unexpecting posture that leads to a beautiful moment…for me.

The truth is, it is hard to sneak up on people who are looking for it. They are too busy paying attention to what is going on around them to fall prey to tactics like mine.

One of the things that I love about Jesus was His willingness to give people a heads up and a warning. As the One who loves us and cares for our lives, He doesn't want things to sneak up on us and catch us off guard. He wants us prepared and engaged. One thing He told us to be aware of is greed.

Most people I know would never describe themselves as *greedy*. But take a moment and notice Jesus words. He tells the crowd to "watch out and be on guard against *all greed...*"

Here is what I know: greed can manifest itself in a lot of ways.

And I've come to realize that greed is no respecter of person. It isn't just a rich people problem. It also isn't just a poor people problem. It's a human condition problem. I think greed is hard to spot in our own lives because of the culture that we live within. Just like a fish that doesn't understand it is swimming in water, life in the West – specifically in America leans toward greed. You can see it in our marketing and in our consumerism. You can see it in the way lives are being crippled with debt in order to "get things" that they actually can't afford. You can see it in the way that media works to create a sense of "missing out" if you don't have

_____.

Greed is all around us.

And if we are honest, greed is in us.

Jesus doesn't want to have His followers overcome by a sneak attack from this thing called greed. So He lovingly gives us a heads up.

To drive the idea further, Jesus reminds us how to measure life.

And what He shares makes every advertising firm uneasy: the measure of your life isn't based in your possessions. This is a huge statement and an important truth. Your possessions don't make you. They don't shape your value or confirm your belonging, or even secure your sense of identity.

I know we all have a tendency to look to *things*. The new car, that outfit, those shoes, that trip, a vacation home…the list can go on and on. None of these things are bad or wrong to have. Where we get ourselves in trouble is when we *look to these things to find security, purpose, comfort, identity, or belonging* that can ultimately only be found in Jesus alone.

You can have garages full of cars, closets full of clothes and shoes, passports full of stamps to incredible destinations traveled…and still be empty.

Watch out for greed.
Jesus offers you a better way to measure your life.

P.S. – We can't take any of it with us when we die anyway… As someone once said, *I've never seen a hearse pulling a U-Haul trailer.*

DAILY PRINCIPLE:
YOU CAN OWN A LOT AND STILL BE
EMPTY WITHOUT JESUS.

DAILY PRACTICE:
CONTEXT: *Put Jesus' Words in context
by reading **Luke 12:13-21***

REFLECT:
*What things stuck out to you from
today?*
*What do you sense Jesus speaking to
you about right now?*

PRAY

DAY
TWENTY

MOST IMPORTANT

*"The most important is Listen, Israel! The Lord
our God, the Lord is one. Love the Lord your
God with all your heart, with all your soul, with
all your mind, and with all your strength. The
second is, Love your neighbor as yourself.
There is no other command greater than
these."*

(Jesus answering a question from a religious leader in
Mark 12:29-31)

If you were to sit down and list out what the
most important things to you were, what would
make the list? Each and every one of us has a
set of priorities and focuses that we live life by.
These priorities serve as a filter for what we
give our time, attention and energy to.

One day, Jesus was approached by a scribe,
who was a religious leader – well versed in
understanding the Old Testament law. He
asked Jesus of all the laws in the Old
Testament, which one was the most important.

I love that Jesus was willing to not only allow
this man to ask a question, but Jesus was also
willing to engage with him in his question.
Jesus quotes from Deuteronomy 6:4-5, known
as the *Shema*. He then references Leviticus
19:18. Jesus takes all of the Law and the

Prophets and summarizes what is most important:

LOVE GOD with all that you are.

LOVE PEOPLE as yourself.

Love God. Love People.

It's simple. But let's be honest for a moment: it's not *easy*.

Jesus is defining for us what is most important in life. In everything that we can do, in all the ways we can use our time, energy and attention, it comes down to loving God with all that I am *and* loving people as myself. Let's unpack this a bit.

I've met a lot of people who have a very individualistic view of how their relationship with God works itself out. "It's just them and Jesus." Here is the problem: if we say we love God with all that we are, it will be reflected in *how* we love others.

Why?

Because God's passion is people. As we read a number of days ago (in John 3:16-17), He loves the world. What does this mean for us? It means that as we grow to love God more, it will be revealed in our interactions and care for others. A deeper love for God will move me to a deeper love for others.

My guess is if you made it this far into this book, love for God is now somewhere on your priority list of life, even if you are still simply seeking to know Jesus – you're making it a priority. But pause and ask yourself: is it *the* priority or *a* priority?

And if you are at a place where God is *the* priority in your life, how is that being reflected in how you are loving other people?

Do you love everyone or do you just love those who are easy to love? You know what I mean…people who think like you, talk like you, vote like you – or are you growing to reveal a God-type love to those who are in need of the love of Jesus that you are here to express to them?

Priorities matter.

Jesus defined His:
LOVE GOD. LOVE PEOPLE.

DAILY PRINCIPLE:
> JESUS DEFINED HIS PRIORITIES
> FOR HIS FOLLOWERS: LOVE GOD.
> LOVE PEOPLE.

DAILY PRACTICE:
> **CONTEXT**: *Put Jesus' Words in context
> by reading* **Mark 12:28-34**

> **REFLECT**:
> *What things stuck out to you from
> today?*
> *What do you sense Jesus speaking to
> you about right now?*

PRAY

DAY
TWENTY-ONE

FOR THE HUNGRY

"For the bread of God is the one who comes down from heaven and gives life to the world." "I am the bread of life…No one who comes to me will ever be hungry, and no one who believes in me will ever be thirsty again."

(Jesus speaking to a crowd of people in **John 6:33, 35**)

Our two boys crossed into their teen years a while ago. When that happened, there was a shift in our house: we started going through a lot more food. We would eat dinner, and an hour later they were making more food, or clearing out the snacks from the pantry. There was an interesting thing that was happening: no matter how much they ate they would get hungry again.

Even though it seems to be more pronounced in our boys, it is the same with every human. We eat, and then we get hungry again.

In the Gospels, Jesus performs an incredible miracle by feeding 5,000 people with a few loaves of bread and a few small fish. Scripture says that the crowd "ate and were satisfied." And then something else happened – they got hungry again. Seeing that Jesus and His disciples had parted, they tracked Jesus down by getting into boats and looking for Him.

When the found Him, they wanted something else to eat.

It is in this backdrop that Jesus provides a significant teaching about who He is and what He came to do.

The people referenced that Moses provided "manna" (a type of bread) for their ancestors while they were traveling through the wilderness. Jesus reminded them that it wasn't Moses, but it was God who had provided it. Then Jesus went on to remind them that God has again provided bread from heaven that would give life to people. And then Jesus says something shocking:

He is that bread. *He* is the bread of life.

The very hunger that each of us feels is a reminder that we have a need. We need and we crave to be filled. Jesus speaks to the crowd who is thinking about their physical appetite and craving, and He uses that to draw them to a spiritual understanding. He is the very thing that they need.

I love what Jesus promises in His words here. Pause and consider their significance for you today. Jesus said that those who come to Him – the Bread of Life – will never be hungry again or thirsty again.

Your physical body will still need nourishment, yes. But your soul will finally find that satisfaction and provision that it constantly craves.

Here is what I know about our appetites: they have an unending ability to crave more. What my unending appetite *needs* is the provision that only an *unlimited* God can provide.

My soul is needy, and so is yours. Because our need is unlimited, we need to look to an unlimited source to provide for our need. We will only find satisfaction in one place: Jesus. So today, run to Him. Receive Him as your Bread of Life. Let Him fill you, nourish you, strengthen you, and bless you. He has an unlimited supply, so when your soul is hungry and needy again later today, tomorrow, or the next day, never forget that you can keep coming to Him as the source that your soul craves and needs.

DAILY PRINCIPLE:

THE SOLUTION TO OUR UNLIMITED APPETITE IS AN UNLIMITED SAVIOR NAMED JESUS.

DAILY PRACTICE:

CONTEXT: *Put Jesus' Words in context by reading* ***John 6:22-44***

REFLECT:
What things stuck out to you from today?
What do you sense Jesus speaking to you about right now?

PRAY

DAY
TWENTY-TWO

WHO IS WHO?

"I am the vine; you are the branches. The one who remains in me and I in him produces much fruit, because you can do nothing without me."

(Jesus speaking to His disciples in **John 15:5**)

As I write this, I am in central Washington looking out across a lake. The sun is shining, and the beauty is astounding. Across the water on the hills opposite of where we are staying are rows and rows of perfectly manicured vineyards. The green of the vines stands out as a vibrant contrast to the surrounding central Washington brown that comes with the season on this side of the Cascade mountains.

Over 2,000 years ago, Jesus was having an important conversation with His students – His disciples that have traveled with Him for the past three years. He is wanting to impart the wisdom and information that they will need to carry His mission forward following His death and resurrection that was just hours away. He gives them a metaphor to help remind them of their connection with Him and the characteristic that He expected of them.

He uses the image of a vineyard.

151

This imagery has deep significance, and we could fill a book with its applications and importance. But today, I want us to consider just a few details with what Jesus speaks to.

First, He clarifies *who is who*. Jesus says He is the vine and we are the branches.

This is important to not glance over or move past too quickly. Here is why: so often, people want to "add Jesus to *their* life", but this isn't what Jesus is describing. The vine is the only way that a branch can survive. The vine doesn't connect to the branch, the branch grows and receives life from the vine. The same is true in our relationship with Jesus. When we come to place our trust in Jesus, we don't simply add a little Jesus compartment to our lives. We don't just give Him a little place in our schedule once a week. We understand that our lives have been radically reoriented around who He is – and that He is our source of life.

Often, I can be guilty of wanting Jesus to be *my* branch. I want Him to produce the fruit that I desire. I want Him to help me accomplish *my dreams and my desires*. But this is not at all what Jesus is describing the relationship to be between Him and His disciples.

Second, Jesus tells us that fruit is a byproduct of abiding or "remaining" in Him. Fruit in our lives should be the natural outgrowth of relationship with Jesus. Fruit doesn't grow through straining, striving, and grunting. Fruit happens because of connection. As true as this is for the vineyards of central Washington, it is true for our lives as we journey with Jesus.

Third, Jesus says something that should stop us in our tracks. Jesus literally says that without Him, we can do *nothing.* He didn't say that without Him it will be hard and challenging. He didn't imply that we will be able to get some things done, but He is actually the cosmic fast pass to all of our hopes and desires.
He says that apart from Him, *we can do nothing.*

This, if I'm being honest, is a little scary. Because I know that there have been many days that I have felt productive, yet I didn't really lean into Him. So if what He is saying is true, what did I actually accomplish?

Today, take a moment to honestly reflect on how you are approaching life in Jesus. Allow the Holy Spirit to illuminate and bring to your attention areas where there is a disconnect and you are more dependent on you than you are on Jesus. Let Him reveal the times and the places that you have acted like Jesus is *your* branch verses Him being the vine for your life. Maybe there are some things that need to be adjusted. Maybe there are some things that need to be pruned. Even though moments like that are not easy, they do lead to fruit. And Jesus loves it when our lives are both faithful and fruitful.

DAILY PRINCIPLE:
APART FROM JESUS I CAN DO NOTHING.

DAILY PRACTICE:
CONTEXT: *Put Jesus' Words in context by reading* ***John 15:1-8***

REFLECT:
What things stuck out to you from today?
What do you sense Jesus speaking to you about right now?

PRAY

DAY
TWENTY-THREE

WATCH!

"Watch! Be alert! For you don't know when the time is coming."

(Jesus speaking to four of His disciples in **Mark 13:33**)

One of the reasons that followers of Jesus live with an unyielding sense of hope regardless of the circumstances going on around them is that we are people who live life through a different lens. We see things different because of the promises of Jesus. These promises were not just ancient truths spoken and now outdated. These promises are alive and are the key to experience life.

We have the promise of forgiveness through what Jesus has accomplished for us, and because of this, we now have gained access to relationship with God that was broken because of sin.

We have the promise of the Spirit now living within us. Jesus revealed in John 7 that the Holy Spirit would fill the lives of His followers.

We also have the promise that Jesus is coming again, and He will set all things right! This is good news, especially as we look at the brokenness and pain that we see in this world. Our King is coming again!

Yet Jesus didn't tell us when this would take place.

For years, people have worked to determine a date. In fact in recent years, there was an individual who purchased adds nationally putting a date for when Jesus was going to return. This is odd when you consider the words that Jesus shared with His disciples: *you don't know when the time is coming.*

Because they didn't know the year, the day or the time, Jesus gave them and gives us a simple instruction: Watch! And Be Alert!

But what does it mean to *watch?*

I have seen some Christians take this to mean live in a constant state of paranoia. But surely this can't be what Jesus was calling us to do. It seems out of alignment that the Prince of Peace would have followers living lives that are in a constant state of low grade freakout.

I have seen others work to look at every single detail to figure out when it *might* happen. And though study and learning is good, I'm not convinced that this is the type of watching and being alert that Jesus was looking for either.

I think what Jesus was getting at was that He desired that His followers would live with a constant expectation that their King was coming again. They would be filled with hope that He wasn't going to leave things as they are forever. When some hear "Watch!", what they hear is a threat – a harsh word to the tune of "you better get your act together or else…"

Instead, I would ask us to consider the intent of Jesus in this moment. Calling His disciples to live with an anticipation and expectation of His return. To remember that they are people of promise – and He is the One who not only makes the promise but is also the fulfiller of it.

Our King is coming again.

So today, take a moment and reflect. Are you living with anticipation and expectation that Jesus is coming again? Are you ready for that? Are you excited for that moment? Are you living each day through the lens of that promise?

DAILY PRINCIPLE:
OUR KING NAMED JESUS IS COMING AGAIN!

DAILY PRACTICE:
CONTEXT: *Put Jesus' Words in context by reading* **Mark 13:32-37**

REFLECT:
What things stuck out to you from today?
What do you sense Jesus speaking to you about right now?

PRAY

_____
_____
_____
_____
_____
_____
_____
_____
_____
_____
_____
_____
_____
_____
_____
_____
_____
_____
_____
_____
_____
_____
_____
_____
_____
_____
_____
_____
_____
_____

DAY
TWENTY-FOUR

EVIDENCE

"By this everyone will know that you are my disciples, if you love one another."

(Jesus speaking to His disciples on the night of His betrayal in **John 13:35**)

Every now and then someone will remark to me about how much one of my kids looks like me, or walks like me. This always puts a smile on my face. I would hope that our kids reflect both their mother and me, since they have our DNA.

In a very similar way, I think Jesus followers should look like Him, since we are carriers of His spiritual DNA. When we put our trust in Jesus, we didn't just become *better* – we became *alive*. And since we are alive in Him and we have received this life from Him, we should reflect His qualities and attributes.

On the night that Jesus was betrayed and handed over to be crucified, He was sharing a meal with His students – His disciples. In this setting He unpacks so many important truths that they will need in the hours and days ahead. One of the things He tells them is that He is giving them a new commandment.

There have been too many times that I have treated God's commandments more like suggestions. My assumption is that I am not the only one. Jesus gives His disciples a new commandment that they are to *love one another as Jesus has loved them.*

Jesus didn't ask them to tolerate one another. He didn't suggest that they would need to at least act like they are getting along in public. He didn't offer clauses or opt out options for those who felt like Jesus was abusing His power.

He simply commanded them: love one another. But then Jesus takes it a step further. He lets the disciples in on a little secret. That they are not just doing this for *Jesus' benefit.* No. Jesus goes on to say that their love will become the *evidence* that they are actually followers of Jesus.

Take a moment to think about a few followers of Jesus you know.

Is the first word that comes to your mind when you think about *why* you know they are followers of Jesus, LOVE?

Sit on that for a moment.

Jesus expected that this would be a characteristic of His disciples. That love would mark them, because His love had marked them. If they were transformed because of

166

Jesus' love, they should live out a transformational love to those around them.

Yet the common caricature portraying Christians in media, movies and shows is a bunch of uptight, judgmental, and hypocritical people who don't live out what they have claimed to receive from Jesus. This is both frustrating and sad.

It frustrates me because I don't think it is a fair assessment of so many faithful followers of Jesus.

It is sad because I too have met many Christians that fit this stereotype.

So, the question is, how do we change that?

The answer is actually quite simple, though it isn't easy: we live out love.

We take Jesus serious with His call to love one another *as He has loved us*. This means that love will be sacrificial and self-giving. It will be generous and gracious. That love will be abundant and applied. When Jesus followers live like this, it becomes evidence that the Gospel is real and that Jesus is good.

DAILY PRINCIPLE:
WHAT IS THE EVIDENCE THAT YOU
ARE REVEALING AS A FOLLOWER
OF JESUS?

DAILY PRACTICE:
CONTEXT: *Put Jesus' Words in context
by reading* **John 13:31-35**

REFLECT:
*What things stuck out to you from
today?*
*What do you sense Jesus speaking to
you about right now?*

PRAY

DAY
TWENTY-FIVE

SALT & LIGHT

"You are the salt of the earth…
You are the light of the world..."

(Jesus teaching a crowd in His Sermon on the Mount in
Matthew 5:13-14)

It is often easy to only think about how following Jesus impacts our lives individually. We think about the gift of grace and mercy that is found only in Jesus, and how it meets us to undo all that our sin has done. We know that we are reconciled to God. That the Spirit now dwells in us. That we have access to God and can come boldly to Him (Hebrews 4:16). We grow to understand that we are now welcomed in as children, and we have a new identity and a new standing.

All of these truths are life changing realities.

In addition to these things, Jesus also reminded His followers of the impact of following Him that would bring transformation *beyond them*.

He uses a powerful image that is sometimes lost on us as modern readers.

One day as He is teaching He tells the crowd that they are "the salt of the earth", and that they are "the light of the world". Salt and Light. Let's dig into this a little deeper.

We live in a time where we can walk into a grocery store and find just about anything we want or need. The idea of waiting for something has nearly been erased from the western paradigm. In fact, we can *preserve* things and get items that would usually be out of season. Something that we take for granted, like refrigeration, did not exist in the time in which Jesus was teaching. So in order to preserve things from going bad and spoiling, they used *salt*.

Salt was a preservative. It fought against the natural decay that would take place in the middle eastern heat. If you wanted something to last, and you wanted to keep it from decaying, you would use salt.

Jesus is reminding the crowd that His followers will be a solution to the decay that was taking place around them. They were to be preservatives in the midst of a world that was suffering from spiritual decay. This matters because as I faithfully follow Jesus, it doesn't impact me – it quite literally impacts the world around me.

Jesus also reminded the crowd that those who follow Him and experience life in His Kingdom would be *light*. Light has a purpose. Light is

transformational. Light is designed to shine and bring illumination. Jesus goes on to say that when you light a lamp, you don't hide it, but you allow it to do its work by transforming the environment and expelling the darkness.
Salt and light. This is what happens as you faithfully follow Jesus.

It is personal, yes! But your faith is also designed to have an impact beyond you.

So, take a moment today and reflect: how is your life being salt and light? Do you notice it? Can others observe it?

Your faith is designed to make a difference. So let that light shine and be a force that partners with Jesus to prevent decay.

DAILY PRINCIPLE:
YOUR FAITH IS DESIGNED TO MAKE
A DIFFERENCE.

DAILY PRACTICE:
CONTEXT: *Put Jesus' Words in context
by reading* **Matthew 5:13-16**

REFLECT:
*What things stuck out to you from
today?*
*What do you sense Jesus speaking to
you about right now?*

PRAY

DAY
TWENTY-SIX

FOR YOUR BENEFIT

"Nevertheless, I am telling you the truth. It is for your benefit that I go away, because if I don't go away the Counselor will not come to you. If I go, I will send him to you."

(Jesus teaching His disciples about the Holy Spirit in **John 16:7**)

Have you ever had that confusing moment where someone was trying to convince you that something was a blessing, when it sounded like a burden?

I remember a number of years ago I was training for a half-marathon. I enjoy distance running, especially when I have a goal in sight. I was talking about the training process that I was in, and my friend looked at me and said the following: I've never seen anyone who actually looks like they are enjoying themselves when they are running. Everyone in the room laughed and agreed, because let's face it: when you are driving and you see someone running on the side of the road, it doesn't look like they are living the dream. Even though I was describing something that I loved to do and felt like it was a blessing to me, my friend simply heard the burden attached.

Jesus' disciples had a similar experience.

In John's gospel we read a long section of scripture where Jesus is teaching His disciples and preparing them for His coming death, resurrection, and departure. He has spent the past three years with them, inviting them to apprentice with Him in learning the ways of His Kingdom. They have come to understand that He is the Messiah, the promised One from the Old Testament prophecies that would undo what humanities sin had set into motion in Genesis 3.

Jesus, in this setting, says something that doesn't sound like a benefit.

He tells His disciples that He is going away. *And it is actually for their good – for their benefit that He is leaving.*

I can almost hear the disciples' questions: "What?! Jesus, how is that going to help us? How is that going to benefit us? You are everything we have been looking for and hoping for? And now you're leaving?"

Jesus explains why this is such a benefit, and not a burden. He tells them that if He goes away, He will send *the Counselor* (the Holy Spirit) to be with us and in us. To the disciples, this would have been shocking information. They understood that in the Old Testament, the Holy Spirit was active. But He only came on specific people at specific times for a specific purpose.

Jesus is revealing something radically different. His followers are all going to have access to the Holy Spirit. Jesus wasn't going to be with them physically, but the Spirit was going to take up residence in their lives, and He would lead them into the truth that they need. This changes everything.

Yes, I mean that and believe that wholeheartedly.

If you are a follower of Jesus, you have the Spirit dwelling in your life. This should change the way we live out our days. This should change how we face hardship and difficulty. This should change how we view prayer. This should change what we believe about what God wants to do *in us* and *through us*.

Please don't take this for granted. The Spirit of God is with you and in you. Right now. In this very moment. Sit with that thought for a second.

How does this truth transform us? How does it change how we show up at work? How does it shift how we parent and how we serve our spouse? How does this impact how we view ourselves and our worth? How does this adjust what we believe about how God desires to work in and through us?

The Holy Spirit is in you if you are a follower of Jesus.

Live life with that awareness.

DAILY PRINCIPLE:
THE HOLY SPIRIT LIVES IN ME, AND
THAT CHANGES EVERYTHING.

DAILY PRACTICE:
CONTEXT: *Put Jesus' Words in context
by reading **John 15:26 - 16:15***

REFLECT:
*What things stuck out to you from
today?*
*What do you sense Jesus speaking to
you about right now?*

PRAY

DAY
TWENTY-SEVEN

GO.

"Go, therefore, and make disciples…"

(Jesus speaking to His disciples after He rose from the dead in **Matthew 28:19**)

Jesus had a plan for His followers. That plan wasn't limited to coming together every so often on a Sunday (when we don't have something else to do). It wasn't that we would pile up hours listening to podcasts or jumping on YouTube to get that latest message from our new favorite preacher. His plan was much more active. His plan was for us to *go*.

The century following Jesus' death and resurrection was filled with ordinary people doing extraordinary things because of the Good News that transformed their life, and the Spirit's work to continue what Jesus had set into motion. The first century was marked by the Church *going* on mission with Jesus.

This is tied to Jesus' final words to His disciples before He ascended to heaven following His resurrection from the grave. He told His disciples that He had received all authority in heaven and on earth through His victorious work on the cross. With that in mind, He called His disciples to *go* into all the world and make disciples of all nations.

There are a few things I think we should consider from this.

First, if we are going to be faithful followers of Jesus, it will include *going*. The Christian life isn't about showing up and sitting through a church gathering, hoping to add a little more biblical information to help you get through next Thursday or to help you live a better life. It is so much more than that. The same hope that met you through the grace of Jesus is needed in the lives of others. And guess who is called to carry and deliver that? No, it's not just your pastor.

It is *you*.

One of the signs that we are growing and active in our faith is seen in our *going*.

Second, Jesus called the disciples to make disciples. This matters. Understand, Jesus didn't give us the call to go and help people make a decision about Him. The decision matters, but it is the starting line, not the finish line. We are called to help move people from that decision to follow Jesus to become fully devoted followers (or disciples) of Him.
And – don't miss this – what is it that makes a disciple?

Jesus didn't give the disciples a program to take around the world. I am all for programs, if they serve the right purpose and accomplish the mission. But we must remember, programs don't make disciples. Disciples make disciples. This is what is so amazing about Jesus' plan. He saved people, calls them to follow Him and become disciples (students of His life and His way of life), that they could go and teach others how to do the same. This is what discipleship actually looks like.

This is where our *going* should lead. In a matter of a few years following the resurrection of Jesus, this news had spread throughout the Roman empire and the greater Mediterranean regions. How did this happen so quickly and effectively? Because disciples of Jesus took their call to *go* seriously.

They didn't have access to resources and technology like we do. But the same Holy Spirit that propelled them in the mission of Jesus is alive and active today. Imagine what we could accomplish if we took Jesus' Words seriously enough to *go*.

DAILY PRINCIPLE:
JESUS INVITES ME TO BE A
DISCIPLE WHO WILL *GO* AND MAKE
OTHER DISCIPLES.

DAILY PRACTICE:
CONTEXT: *Put Jesus' Words in context
by reading* **Matthew 28:16-20**

REFLECT:
*What things stuck out to you from
today?
What do you sense Jesus speaking to
you about right now?*

PRAY

DAY
TWENTY-EIGHT

THE HEART

"Don't let your heart be troubled. Believe in God; believe also in me."

(Jesus speaking to His disciples in **John 14:1**)

If you live life long enough, you will encounter situations and circumstances that have the ability to trouble your heart.

> *An unexpected diagnosis.*
> *The loss of a loved one.*
> *A failed marriage.*
> *A breakdown in relationship with a child.*
> *An addiction that you can't seem to break free from.*
> *The abrupt ending to a career.*

The list could go on and on. We all experience life in this world that will never be the paradise we so often long for it to be. But part of the shared human experience is "*stuff happens*". There is this sense when we encounter moments and seasons like this where we feel that it isn't supposed to be like this. It is as if we are longing for life in the garden before the fall in Genesis 3. There is an ache that we feel, knowing that things are supposed to be different. We long for it. We want it.

Jesus gives us hope.

Consider His simple call to His disciples: "Don't let your heart be troubled…"

Jesus knew that in a matter of time, He would be arrested, suffer, be crucified and die. He knew that this was going to trouble the hearts of the disciples who had given up everything to follow Him the past three years. He knew that they would look at these circumstances and be convinced that it was over. Their hearts would become burdened with grief, thinking that their hope had died with Jesus' final breath.

But Jesus wants them to embrace a greater reality.

Don't let your heart be troubled…Believe…

There are a few important things to recognize from Jesus' words here.

First, we must learn to direct our hearts instead of our hearts directing us. Scripture tells us that our hearts are deceptive (Jeremiah 17:9), and that we should guard them because they end up directing the course of our lives (Proverbs 4:23). Jesus specifically told His followers to *not* allow their hearts to be troubled.

But *how* do we do that? If you are anything like me, chances are that your emotions have gotten the best of you at one time or another.

Maybe you have allowed thing to build up to where they are boiling over and you are now in the passenger seat of your heart and your emotions.

Been there?

Jesus next word is key: **Believe**.

The antidote to not allowing our hearts to be overcome or overwhelmed is leaning into what we believe about God – Father, Son, and Holy Spirit. When I come back to right believing, it is amazing how quickly my outlook changes. At the end of the day, right believing leads us to right behaving. Whenever there is a disconnect in my *behaving,* I need to pause and consider what is the *belief* under the *behavior*?

So, in this moment, pause and consider Jesus' words about not allowing your heart to be troubled. Where are you currently anxious? What has your emotions stirred in an unhealthy way? Where is there a potential disconnect in your belief that is driving a behavior that needs adjustment?

Today is a good day to not allow your heart to be troubled. Why? Because you believe in Jesus.

DAILY PRINCIPLE:
> TODAY IS A GOOD DAY TO NOT ALLOW YOUR HEART TO BE TROUBLED.

DAILY PRACTICE:
> **CONTEXT**: *Put Jesus' Words in context by reading **John 14:1-7***

> **REFLECT**:
> *What things stuck out to you from today?*
> *What do you sense Jesus speaking to you about right now?*

PRAY

DAY
TWENTY-NINE

FIRST THINGS FIRST

"But seek first the kingdom of God and his righteousness, and all these things will be provided for you."

(Jesus teaching about life in His Kingdom in **Matthew 6:33**)

All of us live with a set of priorities that drive the direction and decisions we make in life. Everyone has a set of filters (either by design or by default) that serve us in shaping the choices that directly impact the destination and destiny of our lives.

Consider a few of the following priorities that some people live by:

> *Convenience and Comfort*
> *Control and Influence*
> *Protection and Safety*
> *Risk and Reward*
> *Future*
> *Immediate satisfaction*

The list could go on, but my guess is that something on the above list resonated with a filter that gets used in some of the decisions that you make day to day in how you live your life.

Jesus, as He is talking to the crowd in His Sermon on the Mount addresses something that all of us has faced, is facing or will face at some point in our journey: *worry.* In this section of His teaching, He goes through a list of things that we commonly concern ourselves with.

In the midst of the common worries of life, He gives His listeners an invitation: *trust that God has your best interest in mind and reorient your priorities on what truly matters.* Let's look at these two ideas for a moment.

First, *trust.* It is so much easier to talk about trust and use the language of trust than it is to actually live trust out. Why? Because trust actually requires me to *trust.* It puts the power and control somewhere else and with someone else. And if we are honest, this is really hard for us to do. We end up wrestling with common fears and concerns: *What if it doesn't work out? What if it doesn't happen? What if I don't have enough?*

I get it. The journey of faith presents us countless opportunities to trust. And I know some of you may be thinking right now, "That's great and all…but *trust* doesn't pay the bills." Jesus' words push at the root of our worry and the methods we often use to compensate. The solution He gives us includes actually *trusting God.* He really does have our best interest in mind. He really is aware. He really does care for you and your needs.

But this call to trust leads us to the second part of Jesus' invitation: to reorder and reorient the priorities of our lives. My assumption if you have made it this far into our 31-day journey is that you would say Jesus *is a priority* in your life. But pause for a moment and reflect on what Jesus actually invites us to do.
He doesn't ask to be a priority among many priorities in our lives.

He welcomes us to make Him and His Kingdom *the priority* that all other priorities are ordered from.

This is big.

He invites us to not simply fit Him into the cracks of an overloaded schedule when we can find the time. He isn't asking for us to give Him a little nod every now and then in our schedule, our finances, or our agendas.

He simply states: Seek first…

In your life, what has first place? Is there room where the Holy Spirit is inviting you to reorient and reorder some things?

Today is a good day to put the first things *first*.

DAILY PRINCIPLE:
JESUS IS INVITING ME TO TRUST
HIM AND TO REORDER MY
PRIORITIES.

DAILY PRACTICE:
CONTEXT: *Put Jesus' Words in context
by reading **Matthew 6:25-34***

REFLECT:
*What things stuck out to you from
today?
What do you sense Jesus speaking to
you about right now?*

PRAY

DAY
THIRTY

THIRSTY?

"If anyone is thirsty, let him come to me and drink."

(Jesus speaking in the temple during the Feast of Tabernacles in **John 7:37**)

One of the things that the scriptures continue to point us to is that Jesus is actually the fulfillment of all of the Old Testament promises and prophecies about God's plan to rescue and redeem the world. This matters, because without that perspective in our hearts, we could simply read Jesus' words as little "nuggets of encouragement" for our daily lives. Instead, it is important to recognize the implications of what He is communicating in the context of God's promises being fulfilled.

A great example of this is found in John 7, during one of the great Jewish festivals known as the Feast of Tabernacles. People would travel for miles to Jerusalem to be a part of this great festival. It is in this setting that Jesus peels back the veil so to speak and gives people a glimpse of who He is and the fulfillment that He is setting into motion through His life and His work.

Each day of this festival, the priests would walk a symbolic walk to the pool of Siloam and draw water into a vessel. They would then journey to the steps of the temple and throw the water onto the steps, reminding the people of Israel that God had spoken through His prophets that one day when the Messiah comes, there would be a life-giving river that would flow from the temple to the people bringing renewal and restoration.

On the final day of the festival, while this procession is taking place, Jesus cries out to the crowd: "If anyone is thirsty, let him come to me..." Said another way – I am the true Source that all of this is pointing to. Jesus is confirming that He Himself is the fulfillment of what the people had been hoping and longing for. Jesus goes on to say that those who receive from Him would have a source well up inside of them. He was speaking about the gift of the Spirit taking up residence in the life of His followers.

Pause for a moment and reflect on this:

Jesus is the fulfillment of all the Old Testament promises and prophecies.

Jesus is the true Source that meets the thirsty needs of our lives.

Jesus is the One who will place His Spirit in us. Jesus Himself is the provider of living water, a source that will never run dry.

Understanding this is vital to following Jesus, because He came *for* a purpose and *with* a purpose. He has revealed who He is and why He came.

To take His words and disconnect them from who He is would be a mistake, because His words are pointing us to understand, recognize, and believe something about Him.

So today, listen to His word and respond.

Are you thirsty?

Run to Him. He is the source that will never run dry. He is the One who will fill you with living water.

Rest in that today.

DAILY PRINCIPLE:
JESUS IS THE FULFILLMENT OF
EVERY PROMISE AND PROPHECY.

DAILY PRACTICE:
CONTEXT: *Put Jesus' Words in context
by reading **John 7:10-39***

REFLECT:
*What things stuck out to you from
today?
What do you sense Jesus speaking to
you about right now?*

PRAY

DAY
THIRTY-ONE

THE MOST IMPORTANT QUESTION WE WILL ALL ANSWER

"...who do you say that I am?"

(Jesus asking His disciples a question in **Luke 9:20**)

We have arrived at day 31. You have spent the past few weeks looking at the words of Jesus, reflecting on them, and creating space in your life to grow in your relationship with Him. I hope that there have been moments of encouragement and inspiration. I hope that you have experienced comfort as well as challenge. Mostly I hope that you have grown to love Jesus more and truly see Him for who He is.

But that all leads us to this moment, to face the most important question that we must all answer.

In Luke 9, Jesus is talking with His disciples and He asks them a few questions.

He first asks, "Who do *people* say that I am?"

Note that Jesus isn't asking this because He needs a self-esteem boost or that He is having a momentary narcissistic lapse. He is drawing His disciples into a moment of understanding and confession. They answer with some of the things that people had been saying about Jesus as they heard His teaching and saw His miracles.

But Jesus doesn't leave the disciples there. He then moves to a more personal question. And this is exactly what these last 31 days have been leading us to as well.

I think Jesus understood that you can make observations and assumptions from a distance. He wasn't interested in the opinion of the crowd from a distance. He wanted to know the conviction of those who had drawn close.

So, He makes it personal: "Who do *you* say that I am?"

Right now, in this moment, pause. Consider Jesus sitting with you right now, looking at you with His eyes filled with love, passion, and care for you – and He asks you the same question. He makes it *personal* – Who do *you* say that I am?

He isn't asking what your parents think.

He isn't asking you what your spouse believes.

He isn't wondering how this might impact your social media following.

He isn't probing because He needs a boost in His self-image.

He isn't asking what your pastor believes.

He is asking *you.*

So, what is your answer?

Who do you say Jesus is?

I want you to pause and really think and pray before you pass by that question to quickly. What have you come to believe about Him? What have you experienced from Him?

These questions matter, and so do their answers because they build conviction that is rooted in faith. Developing conviction that is rooted in belief is so important. People can challenge you, argue with you, and even doubt your convictions…but when you experience it yourself, nothing can shake you.

This question "Who do you say that I am?", is a question that every human will have to answer. There are a lot of opinions and ideas about Jesus. But He has revealed through His words who He is.

How you answer that question has an impact on each day of your life and into eternity.

DAILY PRINCIPLE:
WHO DO YOU SAY JESUS IS?

DAILY PRACTICE:
CONTEXT: *Put Jesus' Words in context by reading **Luke 9:18-27***

REFLECT:
What things stuck out to you from today?
What do you sense Jesus speaking to you about right now?

PRAY

CONCLUSION

Life is best when it is *with* Jesus. I am convinced of this.

I continue to learn this lesson each day.

I've met a lot of people throughout the years, and much like myself, they have tried to face life on their own. Through successes and setbacks, through opportunities and opposition, many people have lived a life that is not only disconnected from Jesus, but also completely dependent on what only they can provide for each and every circumstance.

I am convinced there is a better way.

It is found in life *with* Jesus.

My hope and prayer is that over these past 31 days, you have either discovered or rediscovered the beauty of knowing Him. Don't allow yourself to take this for granted: you have the ability to live in an abiding relationship with Jesus. His Words are life. I know that we only scratched the surface of what He said and did. My prayer is that this simple book has served as a catalyst for you in your journey *with* Jesus.

I encourage you to fall in love with His Word.

I encourage you to get plugged in to a local church that is Jesus centered and holds to the authority and inspiration of scripture. Don't simply attend a church, but be a part of the life of the church.

I encourage you to connect with a few other Jesus followers and continue to study His word together regularly. This is what followers of Jesus have been doing together since the first century.

I encourage you to keep a daily rhythm in your life where you encounter Jesus in a real and personal way. This is the key to transformation in our lives.

Don't lose sight of the truth that Jesus loves you, He is for you, and when all else around you fails – He never will!

I will leave you with the following thought from John's Gospel:

> "*But these are written so that you may **believe** that Jesus is the Messiah, the Son of God, and **that by believing you may have <u>life</u> in his name**.*" (John 20:31, CSB – *emphasis added*)

Friend, be confident in this truth:
True life is found only in one place: *With* Jesus.

ABOUT THE AUTHOR

Tyler is the Senior Pastor of Life Center (lifecenter.com), one church with multiple locations and multiple languages in Tacoma, Washington. His passion is to help people KNOW JESUS and MAKE HIM KNOWN.

He and his wife, Amber, have 3 children and have also been involved in foster care. He loves skiing with his family, good coffee, CrossFit, cycling, running and writing.

Connect with Tyler:

> **Blog:**
> tylersollie.com
>
> **Instagram**/ @tylersollie
>
> **Facebook**/ facebook.com/tylersollie
>
> **Twitter**/ @tylersollie